Quote Octopus
Melbourne, Victoria, 3053
Australia
www.quoteoctopus.com

Optimism is the faith that leads to achievement. Nothing can be done without hope and confidence.

Helen Keller

The starting point of all achievement is desire.

Napoleon Hill

Trust yourself. Create the kind of self that you will be happy to live with all your life. Make the most of yourself by fanning the tiny, inner sparks of possibility into flames of achievement.

Golda Meir

Achievement of your happiness is the only moral purpose of your life, and that happiness, not pain or mindless self-indulgence, is the proof of your moral integrity, since it is the proof and the result of your loyalty to the achievement of your values.

Ayn Rand

Happiness lies in the joy of achievement and the thrill of creative effort.

Franklin D. Roosevelt

Without continual growth and progress, such words as improvement, achievement, and success have no meaning.

Benjamin Franklin

You are not here merely to make a living. You are here in order to enable the world to live more amply, with greater vision, with a finer spirit of hope and achievement. You are here to enrich the world, and you impoverish yourself if you forget the errand.

Woodrow Wilson

We cannot seek achievement for ourselves and forget about progress and prosperity for our community... Our ambitions must be broad enough to include the aspirations and needs of others, for their sakes and for our own.

Cesar Chavez

Every successful individual knows that his or her achievement depends on a community of persons working together.

Paul Ryan

Great achievement is usually born of great sacrifice, and is never the result of selfishness.

Napoleon Hill

Happiness does not come from doing easy work but from the afterglow of satisfaction that comes after the achievement of a difficult task that demanded our best.

Theodore Isaac Rubin

My most brilliant achievement was my ability to be able to persuade my wife to marry me.

Winston Churchill

Failures, repeated failures, are finger posts on the road to achievement. One fails forward toward success.

C. S. Lewis

There is no short cut to achievement. Life requires thorough preparation - veneer isn't worth anything.

George Washington Carver

The discipline you learn and character you build from setting and achieving a goal can be more valuable than the achievement of the goal itself.

Bo Bennett

Even a mistake may turn out to be the one thing necessary to a worthwhile achievement.

Henry Ford

Being a father has been, without a doubt, my greatest source of achievement, pride and inspiration. Fatherhood has taught me about unconditional love, reinforced the importance of giving back and taught me how to be a better person.

Naveen Jain

High achievement always takes place in the framework of high expectation.

Charles Kettering

Research shows that there is only half as much variation in student achievement between schools as there is among classrooms in the same school. If you want your child to get the best education possible, it is actually more important to get him assigned to a great teacher than to a great school.

Bill Gates

Optimism is essential to achievement and it is also the foundation of courage and true progress.

Nicholas M. Butler

What is the recipe for successful achievement? To my mind there are just four essential ingredients: Choose a career you love, give it the best there is in you, seize your opportunities, and be a member of the team.

Benjamin Franklin Fairless

Creativity is a great motivator because it makes people interested in what they are doing. Creativity gives hope that there can be a worthwhile idea. Creativity gives the possibility of some sort of achievement to everyone. Creativity makes life more fun and more interesting.

Edward de Bono

With my academic achievement in high school I was accepted rather readily at Princeton and equally as fast at Yale, but my test scores were not comparable to that of my classmates. And that's been shown by statistics, there are reasons for that - there are cultural biases built into testing, and that was one of the motivations for the concept of affirmative action to try to balance out those effects.

Sonia Sotomayor

Those who improve with age embrace the power of personal growth and personal achievement and begin to replace youth with wisdom, innocence with understanding, and lack of purpose with self-actualization.

Bo Bennett

Having children is my greatest achievement. It was my saviour. It switched my focus from the outside to the inside. My children are gifts, they remind me of what's important.

Elle Macpherson

I'll have to say winning the Olympic gold in Atlanta is a crowning achievement, along with the gold in the relay in the same games.

Donovan Bailey

Sir Gordon Richards was the most successful jockey - flat or jumps - there's ever been: champion jockey for 26 years. He set a record of 269 winners in the season 55 years before I broke it. That was my greatest achievement.

Tony McCoy

Meanwhile, parents, students and teachers all report higher satisfaction with charter schools. People like them. They cost less money. They raise the academic achievement of poor kids. Go ahead, get a little enthused.

Maggie Gallagher

The only thing I shall talk about is my sporting achievements at school. My primary sporting achievement at school was that I dodged games for two complete years and was well through the third year before they discovered that I had completely avoided all games.

John Hume

Contentment does not come from achievement.

Paul Henderson

I thought happiness came from achievement.

Paul Henderson

Man has always needed to believe in some form of a continuity of achievement.

Robert Vaughn

I'm sure that some of them will be very hard and I'll have a sense of achievement again, but nothing will mean the same to me - there's no other problem in mathematics that could hold me the way that this one did.

Andrew Wiles

I mean, one thing I know about change is we are not going to close the achievement gap without educators.

Margaret Spellings

I don't think individual achievement in business is the most meaningful way for it to operate.

Michael Eisner

To make the moral achievement implicit in science a source of strength to civilization, the scientist will have to have the cooperation also of the philosopher and the religious teacher.

Arthur Holly Compton

The mean pattern of educational and economic achievement within multi-racial countries such as Canada and the United States has increasingly been found to prove valid internationally.

J. Philippe Rushton

I do think we know that a teacher who knows what he or she is doing, knows their subject matter, and knows how to impart knowledge to kids is a critical piece of closing the achievement gap.

Margaret Spellings

Painting constantly appeared to me as the one and only possible achievement.

Max Beckmann

When I landed the first 900 at the XGames, it was just - it was a personal achievement. It was something that I have strived for for years and years and years, and in a lot of ways had given up on it. But I just didn't think of the resonance that would have.

Tony Hawk

My daughter is my biggest achievement. She is a little star and my life has changed so much for the better since she came along.

Denise Van Outen

With respect to the respective French and German traditions you are no doubt correct, although I am reluctant to see individual achievement reduced to archetypes.

Brian Ferneyhough

I will say that growing up as a kid in an urban environment and having lived in cities all my life, the one achievement that everyone can look forward to is getting the perfect parking spot.

Saul Perlmutter

Getting things straight in your head is a major achievement because there's so much clutter out there. You've got to push aside the static to really hear the music.

Steve Wynn

And, I may add, from what totally unexpected sources come many of those who from the comparatively modest beginning in the chorus rise to the heights of really great achievement in the theatrical profession.

Florenz Ziegfeld

My real achievement is my daughter and my three beautiful grandchildren.

Marilyn Horne

Liberalism regards life as an adventure in which we must take risks in new situation, in which there is no guarantee that the new will always be the good or the true, in which progress is a precarious achievement rather than inevitability.

Morris Raphael Cohen

Liberalism, on the other hand, regards life as an adventure in which we must take risks in new situations, in which there is no guarantee that the new will always be the good or the true, in which progress is a precarious achievement rather than inevitability.

Morris Raphael Cohen

As we take stock of this century of achievement, Ulster Unionists have every reason to feel proud.

David Trimble

The most direct path to achievement whether you're an entrepreneur, a company executive, or a pro soccer player is to be a great performer and a great team member. This is also the secret to a meaningful career and self-fulfillment.

Maynard Webb

Theatre should be a taxing experience: the greatest achievement of a writer is to produce a character who creates anxiety.

Howard Barker

The results indicate that heterogeneity of race and heterogeneity of family educational background can increase the achievement of children from weak educational backgrounds with no adverse effect on children from strong educational backgrounds.

James S. Coleman

In terms of achievement, the pride is very important to me. It keeps me going every day. The money is always second to me.

Weili Dai

Obama sees everything backward. Where Americans see individual achievement, he sees government's work. Where we see failing companies, he sees innovation worth subsidizing. Where we see the need for economic growth, he sees a need for higher taxes.

Reince Priebus

We want to obviously foster a relationship that we're a partner with states; that we all share the same goals of closing the achievement gap, just as the Congress does; and that we're practical and sophisticated enough to understand what they're talking about.

Margaret Spellings

The major economic policy challenges facing the nation today - pick your favorites among the usual suspects of low public and household savings, concerns about educational quality and achievement, high and rising income inequality, the large imbalances between our social insurance commitments and resources - are not about monetary policy.

Timothy Geithner

The principal achievement of Europe is peace, which we often forget about as it has become so taken for granted by Europeans.

Dominique de Villepin

The sort of lifetime achievement stuff that I'm getting now is kind of like Tom Sawyer's funeral because they all know I'm sick. I am getting buildings named after me and awards and stuff.

Sam Simon

Records are just moments of achievement. They're like receipts for work done. Time goes on and people keep playing music.

Bill Laswell

The Vancouver Olympics was the first competition where I completed the short and free programs without any mistakes, and that in itself was a huge achievement.

Yuna Kim

Every scene is a challenge. There are technical challenges, but often it's the simplest challenge where you feel a sense of achievement when you pull it off.

Roger Deakins

We need a tax code that promotes savings, investment, achievement, innovation, and hard work.

Erik Paulsen

I savored my time on top of the podium by watching the American flag rise up out of the crowd as the anthem played, thinking about how every single second of training I've done was for this minute and how many people played a role in my achievement.

Hannah Kearney

As for the single market, the E.U.'s landmark achievement, there is no question that a euro zone breakup would severely disrupt its operation in the short run.

Barry Eichengreen

The failure of women to produce genius of the first rank in most of the supreme forms of human effort has been used to block the way of all women of talent and ambition for intellectual achievement.

Anna Garlin Spencer

I am very optimistic, and I wish that God almighty grants me success to get a qualifying time. Only then can I go to the Olympics. If this happens I will be the first Palestinian athlete to gain a qualifying time. This will be a big achievement.

Nader al-Masri

Whatever he does in office, no man can live up to the high expectations of the world, but we have been changed by his election. Obama's inauguration is a historic global achievement, a major milestone in the journey of a powerful nation.

Des Browne

It's not that I think weddings - or marriages - are letdowns. It's just that I want to see my wedding as one awesome achievement on a continuum of achievements, all of which were, in their way, just as beautiful and profound for having led me to the current one.

Jessi Klein

To be the first Puerto Rican to win a world title in four divisions would be an achievement. Gomez, Benitez, there have been a lot of good fighters from Puerto Rico before me. When I started boxing, Tito Trinidad was our big star.

Miguel Cotto

In both children and adults, there can be a hard-to-deny link between a robust sense of hope and either work productivity or academic achievement.

Jeffrey Kluger

The United States has made a massive effort since the end of the Second World War to secure the dominance of its films in foreign markets - an achievement generally pushed home politically, by writing clauses into various treaties and aid packages.

Fredric Jameson

Although I never marched through the streets shouting for Mao, I do believe that the liberation of China at the end of the 1940s was a wonderful thing and to provide its people with a billion pairs of shoes and trousers was a fantastic achievement.

Henning Mankell

No single achievement in science is possible without the painstaking work of the many hundreds who have built the foundation on which all new work is based.

Polykarp Kusch

Massachusetts children cannot only lead the nation in test scores, they can be competitive with the best in the world. And the gap in achievement among races can virtually disappear.

Mitt Romney

I find it hard to believe that human beings are the crowning achievement of life on earth. Something better than us has to come along.

Douglas Coupland

The miniatures of the Mughal period are really the pinnacle of Indian artistic achievement. And not a single one of those paintings is done by an individual artist.

Salman Rushdie

The accession to power in Pyongyang of Kim Jong Un, son of Kim Jong Il and grandson of Kim Il Sung, is a unique achievement in world politics.

Elliott Abrams

Someone like Roman Polanski comes with a lifetime of achievement, cinematically.

Pierce Brosnan

Men's competitive team sports focus on the balance between individual achievement and team achievement with the emphasis on team achievement.

Warren Farrell

Sanity is surely not about normality in the statistical sense: it is about an eternal and natural idea of the healthy personality - which indeed may be a rare achievement.

Michael Leunig

The fact that we haven't faced another major terrorist attack on American soil since Sept. 11 is a very significant achievement, and one that's easy to forget - it's the dog that doesn't bark.

Alex Berenson

There's a logic today that places a greater value on celebrity the less it is accompanied by actual achievement. I don't think it's possible to touch people's imagination today by aesthetic means.

J. G. Ballard

The real achievement of Woody Allen was that he was making movies that felt very personal, and for a whole group of people, it spoke to them. Then he became an archetype, like Groucho Marx or Chaplin.

Noah Baumbach

One of the things I feel very strong about is the achievement of the Band really being a complete band.

Robbie Robertson

If quantitatively the American achievement is impressive, qualitatively it is somewhat less satisfying.

Irving Babbitt

I have been in Congress for more than a half century. I have lived through times of fear and times of hope. Of despair and of achievement. I have seen our government at its best, but today I fear that we see our government at its worst.

Robert Byrd

To be the most successful male from 'The X Factor' is a big achievement, and I'm chuffed with that.

Olly Murs

Once you've experienced the warmth of an audience, the achievement of getting your first laugh, and entertaining them, singing or playing piano, it just keeps it all going.

Bruce Forsyth

It's become unfashionable to celebrate political achievement, and Labour achievement even less so. And it's positively uncouth to be proud of something that this Labour government is doing. So, slam me for saying so, but I'm really proud of the NHS.

Lucy Powell

I don't think I've done any profound work yet... People ask me, 'How would you want to be remembered?' I tell them I don't want to be remembered! I'm not here to become a Madhubala or receive a Lifetime Achievement Award. I'm not that kind of a person. And I'm not brash about it; it's just the way I am.

Bipasha Basu

I had this big thing about guitar harmonies. I wanted to be the first to put proper three-part harmonies onto a record. That was an achievement.

Brian May

I saw 'Avatar' and liked it very much. It was a great achievement.

Bernardo Bertolucci

I'm very comfortable with the idea of there being late bloomers, and for me, of course, there's no difficulty at all in the way that I think of talent and achievement and so on.

Daniel Tammet

The biological factors underlying race differences in sports have consequences for educational achievement, crime and sexual behavior.

J. Philippe Rushton

It's nice to get any awards, whether it's lifetime achievement or the Keith Richards award for being alive one more year.

Randy Bachman

It is clear from all these data that the interests of teenagers are not focused around studies, and that scholastic achievement is at most of minor importance in giving status or prestige to an adolescent in the eyes of other adolescents.

James S. Coleman

I think that in itself is kind of an amazing achievement to be able to say that your full-time career is in any creative arts, let alone a show that has kept people interested for coming on four seasons and hopefully more.

Anna Paquin

I miss that sensation of a small achievement feeling like a really big deal.

Gavin DeGraw

The film was fair to his musical achievement and gave him every opportunity to explain himself.

Martin Bashir

The way I look at myself, the biggest achievement in my eyes - forget winning trophies or scoring in World Cups - is that I'm still at a top club playing at a really high standard having been almost two different players.

Michael Owen

Governments cannot assume or expect that the ECB will always facilitate their funding independently of the achievement of their fiscal and other policy objectives.

Lucas Papademos

The thing I do, really, is a communication with audiences more than any achievement through records.

Richard Thompson

We have had such a letter movement on two occasions in Denmark when more than a quarter of the adult Danish population participated. Such an achievement, however, demands a really great effort and also a great deal of money.

Fredrik Bajer

For the first time in 15 years, Georgia this winter has its electric power guaranteed without deficit. This is a historic achievement.

Mikheil Saakashvili

I knew very little or nothing about the Olympics. Having qualified was itself a big achievement for me, and then being there was quite overwhelming. Although I lost in the opening round, but the fact that I fought well was enough for me to take away from Athens.

Vijender Singh

First of all, just to get Diner made would have been an achievement in that I got a chance to direct.

Barry Levinson

You are Americans. You love this country. Together we are entrusted with the principles that represent mankind's greatest political and social achievement.

Paul Tsongas

It is exciting to work with students thinking about issues of the day, from closing the achievement gap to finding a cure for cancer.

Freeman A. Hrabowski III

People seem to think that life began with the achievement of personal independence.

Katharine Anthony

The hardest achievement in acting - in my opinion, anyway - is nailing a role that absolutely nobody else could have played. Pacino owned Michael Corleone... but DeNiro could have owned it as well. Who else, though, but Val Kilmer could have nailed Jim Morrison? Does anyone besides Will Ferrell pull off Ron Burgundy?

Bill Simmons

I have been working for over 30 years and am always wondering about where I am and where I am going. It does not stop and become a fixed event of achievement.

Maira Kalman

I grew up in a socialist country. And I have seen what that does to people. There is no hope, no freedom. No pride in achievement.

Thomas Peterffy

If the story is good enough, if it's imaginative enough, if it's moving enough it is going to reach deeper than the level of sheer information and change somebody's life two degrees. That is an enormous achievement.

David Remnick

It is commonly asserted and accepted that Paradise Lost is among the two or three greatest English poems; it may justly be taken as the type of supreme poetic achievement in our literature.

John Drinkwater

Emmys are wonderful and I'm thrilled to death that I have mine. But they're representative of a specific achievement, where this sort of thing is representative of how you've grown in your own industry.

Dinah Shore

The cognitive skills prized by the American educational establishment and measured by achievement tests are only part of what is required for success in life. Character skills are equally important determinants of wages, education, health and many other significant aspects of flourishing lives.

James Heckman

To have united the purposes of an entire Nation, is the great historical achievement of the man in whose strong hands our President has placed the fate of our people.

Gustav Krupp

It will be hard for us and it will be an achievement just to get out of the group stages and through to the quarterfinals, but I am personally dreaming of reaching the final!

Andriy Shevchenko

Enacted under President George W. Bush's administration with the promise to focus on individual student achievement and overall school performance, No Child Left Behind was heralded as groundbreaking. And in some ways, it was.

John Kline

Democracy is fatal for the arts; it leads only to chaos or the achievement of new and lower common denominators of quality.

Walter Legge

Only in North America is it regarded as a major achievement to speak one language moderately well.

Richard Pound

If literary terms were about artistic merit and not the rules of convenience, about achievement and not safety, the term 'realism' would be an honorary one, conferred only on work that actually builds unsentimental reality on the page, that matches the complexity of life with an equally rich arrangement in language.

Charles J. Shields

Being solitary is being alone well: being alone luxuriously immersed in doings of your own choice, aware of the fullness of your won presence rather than of the absence of others. Because solitude is an achievement.

Alice Koller

Never mistake activity for achievement.

John Wooden

The important achievement of Apollo was demonstrating that humanity is not forever chained to this planet and our visions go rather further than that and our opportunities are unlimited.

Neil Armstrong

I don't measure America by its achievement but by its potential.

Shirley Chisholm

Spectacular achievement is always preceded by unspectacular preparation.

Robert H. Schuller

Happiness is that state of consciousness which proceeds from the achievement of one's values.

Ayn Rand

Nothing stops the man who desires to achieve. Every obstacle is simply a course to develop his achievement muscle. It's a strengthening of his powers of accomplishment.

Thomas Carlyle

You should take some responsibility for the way you present yourself. But you should not be hung up on your looks, whether you are ugly or handsome, because it isn't an achievement.

Christopher Reeve

We are the only country in the world that has taken people from so many different backgrounds, which is a great achievement by itself, but an even greater achievement is that we have turned all of that variety and diversity into unity.

Lamar Alexander

The greatest achievement of the human spirit is to live up to one's opportunities and make the most of one's resources.

Luc de Clapiers

Over the years, I've given myself a thousand reasons to keep running, but it always comes back to where it started. It comes down to self-satisfaction and a sense of achievement.

Steve Prefontaine

A dream becomes a goal when action is taken toward its achievement.

Bo Bennett

Life is hard, and a lot of people come home tired from work. If they're gonna spend half an hour reading, they want some entertainment and a sense of achievement. So that's what I give them. That's all I'm trying to do. Is that really so wrong?

James Patterson

I would say my greatest achievement in life right now - my greatest achievement period is - and I'm still trying to achieve it - is to be a wonderful father to my kids.

Bo Jackson

Let freedom reign. The sun never set on so glorious a human achievement.

Nelson Mandela

There is no personal achievement in being born beautiful.

Loretta Young

I always liked my teachers, and I was in a lot of after-school projects. I was a Girl Scout until my senior year, when I couldn't be a Girl Scout anymore. I was in clubs like Junior Achievement, and I ran track and field. My grades were good, but then toward 11th grade they were nothing. I always went to summer school.

Amy Sedaris

The most splendid achievement of all is the constant striving to surpass yourself and to be worthy of your own approval.

Denis Waitley

The greatest achievement was at first and for a time a dream. The oak sleeps in the acorn, the bird waits in the egg, and in the highest vision of the soul a waking angel stirs. Dreams are the seedlings of realities.

James Allen

Every great work, every big accomplishment, has been brought into manifestation through holding to the vision, and often just before the big achievement, comes apparent failure and discouragement.

Florence Scovel Shinn

Sleep makes people calmer, more alert, less fearful - just plain happier, or so I see around me and in me. I am sure that if this great nation were to concentrate on getting more sleep, we would be a happier, more confident people, and that by itself would be a major achievement.

Ben Stein

Definiteness of purpose is the starting point of all achievement.

W. Clement Stone

The final wisdom of life requires not the annulment of incongruity but the achievement of serenity within and above it.

Reinhold Niebuhr

It is probably not love that makes the world go around, but rather those mutually supportive alliances through which partners recognize their dependence on each other for the achievement of shared and private goals.

Fred Allen

Happiness does not lie in happiness, but in the achievement of it.

Fyodor Dostoevsky

Academic achievement was something I'd always sought as a form of reward. Good grades pleased my parents, good grades pleased my teachers; you got them in order to sew up approval.

Caroline Knapp

Badges mean nothing in themselves, but they mark a certain achievement and they are a link between the rich and the poor. For when one girl sees a badge on a sister Scout's arm, if that girl has won the same badge, it at once awakens an interest and sympathy between them.

Juliette Gordon Low

Pretension is a poor joke that you play on yourself. Snap out of it. Recognise your strengths, work on your weaknesses. Real achievement is liking what you see in the mirror every morning.

Virat Kohli

Desire is the starting point of all achievement, not a hope, not a wish, but a keen pulsating desire which transcends everything.

Napoleon Hill

You have to wonder at times what you're doing out there. Over the years, I've given myself a thousand reasons to keep running, but it always comes back to where it started. It comes down to self-satisfaction and a sense of achievement.

Steve Prefontaine

Contentment does not come from achievement. It comes from a relationship with the Lord.

Paul Henderson

Personal relationships are the fertile soil from which all advancement, all success, all achievement in real life grows.

Ben Stein

I am a person who always tries not to be easily influenced by position or achievement. I thank God for the fact that I can share more kindness and a good quality of life through the popularity. Not for the popularity itself.

Mario Teguh

For unflagging interest and enjoyment, a household of children, if things go reasonably well, certainly all other forms of success and achievement lose their importance by comparison.

Theodore Roosevelt

Ultimately, my greatest achievement is maintaining my career while sustaining a happy marriage and kids.

Melina Kanakaredes

Simplicity is the final achievement. After one has played a vast quantity of notes and more notes, it is simplicity that emerges as the crowning reward of art.

Frederic Chopin

This is what America is about when it comes to understanding that it is equal opportunity versus equal achievement. Each and every one of us has the opportunity for greatness in this country.

Allen West

When I went to college, as much as my parents emphasized academic achievement, they emphasized marriage even more. They told me that the most eligible women marry young to get a 'good man' before they are all taken.

Sheryl Sandberg

If you fear making anyone mad, then you ultimately probe for the lowest common denominator of human achievement.

Jimmy Carter

A strong accountability system needs to broaden, not narrow, the curriculum. That cannot happen if you only have accountability without adequate school funding. Until Tallahassee understands the need to raise the bar as well as the financial investment, Florida will continue to celebrate mediocrity at the expense of true achievement.

Dan Gelber

The higher the social class of other students the higher any given student's achievement.

James S. Coleman

I arise full of eagerness and energy, knowing well what achievement lies ahead of me.

Zane Grey

Not only will this make you treat each moment more preciously, but you will be more patient with yourself and with others, recognizing that there are millions of moments on the path to any worthwhile achievement.

Menachem Mendel Schneerson

Achievement is not always success, while reputed failure often is. It is honest endeavor, persistent effort to do the best possible under any and all circumstances.

Orison Swett Marden

All personal achievement starts in the mind of the individual. Your personal achievement starts in your mind. The first step is to know exactly what your problem, goal or desire is.

W. Clement Stone

The roots of true achievement lie in the will to become the best that you can become.

Harold Taylor

Proving I'm a good mother is the one achievement I'm most proud of. It's brought out the best in me.

Sheena Easton

My greatest achievement so far is that I've been able to continue with my normal life. I love what I do, but more so, I'm glad to have people who care about me close by.

Kim Smith

The silent killer of all great men and women of achievement - particularly men, I don't know why, maybe it's the testosterone - I think it's narcissism. Even more than hubris. And for women, too. Narcissism is the killer.

James Woods

The journey that I have undertaken, meeting people from all walks of life and learning from them, has been my biggest achievement.

Aamir Khan

I quite like the idea of family. That's probably the greatest achievement in the world. I've got a lot to achieve workwise - I'd love to direct - but family would be good.

Matt Smith

Think of success as a game of chance in which you have control over the odds. As you begin to master concepts in personal achievement, you are increasing your odds of achieving success.

Bo Bennett

With my academic achievement in high school, I was accepted rather readily at Princeton and equally as fast at Yale, but my test scores were not comparable to that of my classmates. And that's been shown by statistics, there are reasons for that.

Sonia Sotomayor

Women don't take enough risks. Men are just 'foot on the gas pedal.' We're not going to close the achievement gap until we close the ambition gap.

Sheryl Sandberg

The Nobel Peace Prize is a powerful message. A durable peace is not a single achievement, but an environment, a process and a commitment.

Mohamed ElBaradei

To obfuscate the reconstruction of the effect - when a magician is fooled by another magician doing magic. In my career that's not been the major passion, but it's been the passion of a number of my mentors. The crowning achievement for them would be to create magic good enough to fool other magicians.

Ricky Jay

It is extraordinary how safe flying has become. You are now statistically more likely to be elected president of the United States in your lifetime than you are to die in a plane crash. What an amazing achievement as a society! But what we end up focusing on are the catastrophic failures that are incredibly rare but happen every now and then.

Steven Johnson

But the first the general public learned about the discovery was the news of the destruction of Hiroshima by the atom bomb. A splendid achievement of science and technology had turned malign. Science became identified with death and destruction.

Joseph Rotblat

In an ideal world, nobody's work would be just about the money. People could pursue excellence in what they do, take pride in achievement, and derive meaning from knowing that their work improved the lives of others.

Barry Schwartz

Nothing stops the man who desires to achieve. Every obstacle is simply a course to develop his achievement muscle. It's a strengthening of his powers of accomplishment.

Eric Butterworth

But the perception of life as an organic unity is a slow achievement, and depends for its growth on a people's entry into the main current of world-events.

Muhammad Iqbal

Part of the issue of achievement is to be able to set realistic goals, but that's one of the hardest things to do because you don't always know exactly where you're going, and you shouldn't.

George Lucas

Honorary degrees and lifetime achievement awards are very encouraging. I know that it might sound strange that a writer who has published many books still needs encouragement, but this is true.

Joyce Carol Oates

Helping someone come to a saving knowledge of Christ is the greatest achievement possible.

Charles Stanley

The salary of the chief executive of a large corporation is not a market award for achievement. It is frequently in the nature of a warm personal gesture by the individual to himself.

John Kenneth Galbraith

Not in achievement, but in endurance, of the human soul, does it show its divine grandeur and its alliance with the infinite.

Edwin Hubbel Chapin

Inductive reason, which alone makes man master of his environment, is an achievement; and when once born it must be reinforced by inhibiting the growth of other modes of knowledge.

Muhammad Iqbal

Grades are almost completely relative, in effect ranking students relative to others in their class. Thus extra achievement by one student not only raises his position, but in effect lowers the position of others.

James S. Coleman

During the decades after Brown v. Board of Education there was terrific progress. Tens of thousands of public schools were integrated racially. During that time the gap between black and white achievement narrowed.

Jonathan Kozol

Like the skyscraper, the automobile, and the motion-picture palace, neon signs once symbolized popular hopes for a new era of technological achievement and commercial abundance. From the 1920s to the 1950s, neon-lit streets pulsed with visual excitement from Vancouver to Miami.

Virginia Postrel

Increased physical activity during the school day can help children's attention, classroom behavior, and achievement test scores. Meanwhile, the decline of play is closely linked to ADHD; behavioral problems; and stunted social, cognitive, and creative development.

Darell Hammond

I think the sense of family and family achievement, plus the discipline which I received there from that one-room school were really very helpful in what I did later on.

Alan Shepard

One thing I like about Zen. It doesn't believe in achievement.

Agnes Martin

Revolution did not necessarily involve sanguinary strife. It was not a cult of bomb and pistol. They may sometimes be mere means for its achievement.

Bhagat Singh

Achievement brings its own anticlimax.

Maya Angelou

Without failure there is no achievement.

John C. Maxwell

Music to me is mankind's greatest possible achievement because look at all the good it does.

Henry Rollins

Immediately after 11 September, the U.S. closed down the Somali charitable network Al-Barakaat on grounds that it was financing terror. This achievement was hailed one of the great successes of the 'war on terror.' In contrast, Washington's withdrawal of its charges as without merit a year later aroused little notice.

Noam Chomsky

Periods of tranquillity are seldom prolific of creative achievement. Mankind has to be stirred up.

George Santayana

Mere longevity is a good thing for those who watch Life from the side lines. For those who play the game, an hour may be a year, a single day's work an achievement for eternity.

Helen Hayes

By any reasonable measure of achievement, the faith of the Enlightenment thinkers in science was justified.

E. O. Wilson

To become Christ-like is the only thing in the whole world worth caring for, the thing before which every ambition of man is folly and all lower achievement vain.

Henry Drummond

Perfectionism is not the same thing as striving to be our best. Perfectionism is not about healthy achievement and growth; it's a shield.

Brene Brown

The proud depend upon the world to tell them whether they have value or not. Their self-esteem is determined by where they are judged to be on the ladders of worldly success. They feel worthwhile as individuals if the numbers beneath them in achievement, talent, beauty, or intellect are large enough.

Ezra Taft Benson

Periods of tranquility are seldom prolific of creative achievement. Mankind has to be stirred up.

Alfred North Whitehead

Peace is not the product of a victory or a command. It has no finishing line, no final deadline, no fixed definition of achievement. Peace is a never-ending process, the work of many decisions.

Oscar Hammerstein II

It's a historical phenomenon that in 250 years, a nation could move from a colony into the most prosperous nation of the world and the leader of the world. It is indeed an achievement, a tribute to the talent of the American nation, the American people and an optimal political and economic system.

Vladimir Putin

Productive achievement is a consequence and an expression of health and self-esteem, not its cause.

Nathaniel Branden

It's crucial that I kind of keep up, without drifting into the backslapping land of cliche and lifetime achievement awards.

Robert Plant

My greatest achievement is being able to write records that are real snapshots of what's going in my life. I won't repeat myself for the sake of commerce, or to please other people.

Alanis Morissette

Father was the eldest son and the heir apparent, and he set the standard for being a Rockefeller very high, so every achievement was taken for granted and perfection was the norm.

David Rockefeller

Great players are willing to give up their own personal achievement for the achievement of the group. It enhances everybody.

Kareem Abdul-Jabbar

A good game gives us meaningful accomplishment - clear achievement that we don't necessarily get from real life. In a game, you've beaten level four, the boss monster is dead, you have a badge, and now you have a super laser sword. Real life isn't like that, right?

Jesse Schell

Thought is the original source of all wealth, all success, all material gain, all great discoveries and inventions, and of all achievement.

Claude M. Bristol

Companies in the East put a lot more emphasis on human relationships, while those from the West focus on the product, the bottom line. Westerners appear to have more of a need for achievement, while in the East there's more need for affiliation.

Daniel Goleman

My proudest achievement has been the success of the shows and artists I have been involved with, because they were made in Britain.

Simon Cowell

I know that bands that haven't put out a record for 10 years are playing to 20,000 people a night. But that's not the achievement.

Robert Plant

We are deeply conditioned against unconditionality because we've been told in a thousand different ways that accomplishment always precedes acceptance, that achievement always precedes approval.

Tullian Tchividjian

I really admire people who have long-distance relationships. It's an incredible achievement. I couldn't do it.

Rita Ora

Unfortunately, the real achievements of children on the ground became debased and devalued because Labor education secretaries sounded like Soviet commissars praising the tractor production figures when we know that those exams were not the rock-solid measures of achievement that children deserve.

Michael Gove

Achievement results from work realizing ambition.

Adam Ant

The lessons I learned from my mother and her friends have guided me through death, birth, loss, love, failure, and achievement, on to a Fulbright scholarship and Harvard Business School. They taught me to believe that anything was possible. They have proven to be the strongest family values I could ever have imagined.

Gayle Tzemach Lemmon

The only achievement I am really proud of is the friends I have made in this community.

Gary Cooper

If there was any one achievement, it would be that we've have done it on our own terms.

Alex Lifeson

I want to say with the utmost of sincerity, not as a Republican, but as an American, that I have great respect for Senator

Obama's historic achievement to become his party's nominee, not because of his color, but with indifference to it.

Mike Huckabee

Your greatest achievement is to love me.

Prince Charles

On the basis of biological, sociological, and historical knowledge, we should recognize that the individual self is subject to death or decay, but the sum total of individual achievement, for better or worse, lives on in the immortality of The Larger.

Hu Shih

The more specific and measurable your goal, the more quickly you will be able to identify, locate, create, and implement the use of the necessary resources for its achievement.

Charles J. Givens

Use missteps as stepping stones to deeper understanding and greater achievement.

Susan L. Taylor

I have no time for specialized concerns, working themes or variations that lead to mastery... I like the indefinite, the boundless; I like continual uncertainty. Other qualities may be more conducive to achievement, publicity, success; but they are all outworn - as outworn as ideologies, opinions, concepts and names for things.

Gerhard Richter

Well, perhaps the greatest achievement, and we didn't know it at the time, was we held an Earth Day in 1970, and out of that Earth Day a lot of students got involved in saving the environment, or trying to.

Pete McCloskey

There is no finer sensations in life that which comes with victory over one's self. Go forward to a goal of inward achievement, brushing aside all your old internal enemies as you advance.

Vash Young

Not everyone realises that to write a really good piece of journalism is at least as demanding intellectually as the achievement of any scholar.

Max Weber

I do not equate productivity to happiness. For most people, happiness in life is a massive amount of achievement plus a massive amount of appreciation. And you need both of those things.

Timothy Ferriss

Just as an individual's ability to delay gratification at a young age is a powerful predictor of future academic and professional achievement, discipline is also central to the long-run economic health of nations.

Peter Blair Henry

Meeting Stevie Wonder was a massive, lifetime achievement for me. He's one of the sweetest people. I sense a kindred spirit in him, and I hope he'd say the same. Actually, he did.

Hunter Hayes

My father's biggest achievement was to motivate the South Korean people, to show them we could become prosperous if we worked hard. He taught me to love my country, and serve my country.

Park Geun-hye

You cannot compare your athletic achievement to the importance of children and giving them a safe environment in which to grow up and enjoy life.

Steffi Graf

The great achievement of the Catholic Church lay in harmonizing, civilizing the deepest impulses of ordinary, ignorant people.

Kenneth Clark

Periods of cooperation between political parties shouldn't be taken for granted; they are a stunning human achievement.

Paul Bloom

But all actors go through the process, it's hit and miss, you have achievement and failure.

Thomas Haden Church

There is no tragedy more woeful than the victory of hate, nor any attainment so hopelessly barren as the sterility of that achievement; for hate is finality, and finality is the greatest evil which can happen in a world of movement.

James Stephens

There's a great sense of achievement, testosterone, fun, being able to live out your masculinity when you play an action role or an action-adventure or a real tough-guy role.

Gerard Butler

What college is all about is some kind of 4-year game about who is going to end up with the highest grades. And I don't mean to say that academic achievement isn't important. But it is, after all, a means to an end.

Derek Bok

May we all, as a nation of believers, fight for the achievement of America; may we make sacrifices worthy of those proud men and women who fought for us, labored for us, bled soil from the beaches of Normandy to the fields of Gettysburg for us.

Cory Booker

Among all the 'awards' that I have hitherto collected, I consider the title of 'patita' or 'fallen woman' to be the highest. This is an achievement of my long-struggling life as a writer and as a woman.

Taslima Nasrin

Immortality is not a gift, Immortality is an achievement; And only those who strive mightily Shall possess it.

Edgar Lee Masters

I was desperately shy when I was wee. Totally lacked confidence socially. When I look back at school photographs, I'm always the one shrinking in the back. What I really wanted to do was become a writer, and I don't think the residue of that has ever gone away. I still feel the ultimate achievement would be to write a novel.

Anne-Marie Duff

Fame is like the dessert that comes with your achievements - it's not an achievement in itself, but sometimes it can overpower the work.

Adam Clayton

And in terms of their crown jewel legislative achievement: who knew that when asked, 'will government impose a new federal mandate requiring middle class Americans to buy health insurance whether they can afford it or not?' The answer would be 'Yes we can!'

Artur Davis

Innocence of heart and violence of feeling are necessary in any kind of superior achievement: The arts cannot exist without them.

Louise Bogan

The moral and social aspiration proper to American life is, of course, the aspiration vaguely described by the word democratic; and the actual achievement of the American nation points towards an adequate and fruitful definition of the democratic ideal.

Herbert Croly

You must intensify and render continuous by repeatedly presenting with suggestive ideas and mental pictures of the feast of good things, and the flowing fountain, which awaits the successful achievement or attainment of the desires.

Claude M. Bristol

To participate in a World Cup is a great honour and achievement. I've played in three World Cups. The whole world watches you during a World Cup and expects you to play innings to win games for your country.

Virender Sehwag

The educational resources provided by a child's fellow students are more important for his achievement than are the resources provided by the school board.

James S. Coleman

I didn't even have a clear idea of why I wanted to go to Oxford - apart from the fact I had fallen in love with the architecture.

It certainly wasn't out of some great sense of academic or intellectual achievement. In many ways, my education only began after I'd left university.

Alan Bennett

As we talk about the need to foster academic achievement, we must recognize and reward those who strive academically, just as we honor athletic champions. Meeting the President of the United States is just the honor we should bestow on our academic champions.

Brad Sherman

The false pride of perennial celebration, of wearing flag lapel pins while betraying the values that the flag stands for, is like the self-esteem curriculum for toddlers, where everything is praised and no achievement ultimately has meaning.

Anne-Marie Slaughter

I know that people will remember me as Miss Universe because it was my first great achievement, but I still have my whole career ahead of me.

Alicia Machado

It was in Cardiff, and the cast was 60 per cent Welsh-speaking. It's the first time I've walked into a rehearsal room speaking my mother tongue, which in itself was a breath of fresh clean air from the Welsh mountains. Singing Hans Sachs is always a milestone, but I was happy to be part of such an achievement, not personally but as a company.

Bryn Terfel

And yet the Nobel Prizes, in singling out individuals, have done a great deal of good in pointing up to the world as a whole and setting forth clearly goals for achievement.

Willard Libby

Dissatisfaction with possession and achievement is one of the requisites to further achievement.

John Hope

If you ask me why I've succeeded, it's because I was in the Royal Marines. You have this unbelievable sense of achievement and of overcoming adversity. That's the confidence it breeds.

Brian McDermott

Coming to understand a painting or a symphony in an unfamiliar style, to recognize the work of an artist or school, to see or hear in new ways, is as cognitive an achievement as learning to read or write or add.

Nelson Goodman

There is nothing incompatible about laughter and demons, nor about athletic achievement and depression. Mike Flanagan made me laugh, too. But mostly, he made me brave.

Jane Leavy

This homage has been rendered not to me - for the Polish soil is fertile and does not lack better writers than me - but to the Polish achievement, the Polish genius.

Henryk Sienkiewicz

Mother Teresa's detractors have accused her of overemphasizing Calcuttans' destitution and of coercing conversion from the defenseless. In the context of lost causes, Mother Teresa took on battles she knew she could win. Taken together, it seems to me, the criticisms of her work do not undermine or topple her overall achievement.

Bharati Mukherjee

If I were to look back at my career, I think my greatest achievement is very simple. I've been able to make choices where I could glorify God.

Roma Downey

The size of your accomplishments, the quality of your achievement, will depend very largely on how big a man you see in yourself, what sort of image you get of your possible self, yourself at your best.

Orison Swett Marden

There are two kinds of people; those who are always well and those who are always sick. Most of the evils of the world come from the first sort and most of the achievement from the second.

Louis Dudek

Desire is creation, is the magical element in that process. If there were an instrument by which to measure desire, one could foretell achievement.

Willa Cather

Passion is the driver of achievement in all fields. Some people love doing things they don't feel they're good at. That may be because they underestimate their talents or haven't yet put the work in to develop them.

Ken Robinson

I have one piece of advice for those of you who want to receive the Lifetime Achievement Award: Start early!

Shirley Temple

I hadn't realized quite how extraordinary Charles Lindbergh's achievement was in flying the Atlantic alone. He had never flown over open water before, but he flew straight to Dingle Bay in Ireland and then on to Paris, exactly as planned.

Bill Bryson

There's no question that a great teacher can make a huge difference in a student's achievement, and we need to recruit, train and reward more such teachers. But here's what some new studies are also showing: We need better parents. Parents more focused on their children's education can also make a huge difference in a student's achievement.

Thomas Friedman

The American economic, political, and social organization has given to its citizens the benefits of material prosperity, political liberty, and a wholesome natural equality; and this achievement is a gain, not only to Americans, but to the world and to civilization.

Herbert Croly

It is this conception of the unity of the human career which is perhaps the greatest achievement of historical study, since it gained a place analogous to that of natural science.

James Henry Breasted

It's very confusing when fame comes early on in your career. You get a little bit bent out of shape in terms of what's important. Fame is like the dessert that comes with your achievements - it's not an achievement in itself, but sometimes it can overpower the work.

Adam Clayton

Often, when you've reached a very high level of achievement, you almost become paralyzed by the idea that anything you might do might be imperfect. Perfection is just the striving, the effort, the struggle, but it's hard to remember that.

Gelsey Kirkland

The country that consistently ranks among the highest in educational achievement is Finland. A rich country, but education is free. Germany, education is free. France, education is free.

Noam Chomsky

Praise your children more than you correct them. Praise them for even their smallest achievement.

Ezra Taft Benson

I guess that's one achievement I'm really proud of. Saving Chrysler was more than jobs, more than shareholder value. Saving Chrysler was a good idea for the whole country.

Lee Iacocca

Even the mundane task of washing dishes by hand is an example of the small tasks and personal activities that once filled people's daily lives with a sense of achievement.

B. F. Skinner

Take your message of equality of achievement, take your message of economic dependency, take your message of enslaving the entrepreneurial will and spirit of the American people somewhere else.

Allen West

I was motivated to improve the U.S. strategy of going back to the moon in 1985. That's a long time ago. Going back to the moon would be a great achievement for tourism adventure flights.

Buzz Aldrin

Nuclear energy is the scientific achievement of the Iranian nation.

Mahmoud Ahmadinejad

I sometimes wonder how many of these lifetime achievement awards you can accept before you have to do the decent thing and die.

James Taylor

Success has always been easy to measure. It is the distance between one's origins and one's final achievement.

Michael Korda

A successful individual typically sets his next goal somewhat but not too much above his last achievement. In this way he steadily raises his level of aspiration.

Kurt Lewin

But no nation can base its survival and development on luck and prayers alone while its leadership fritters away every available opportunity for success and concrete achievement.

Ibrahim Babangida

Jazz music is America's past and its potential, summed up and sanctified and accessible to anybody who learns to listen to, feel, and understand it. The music can connect us to our earlier selves and to our better selves-to-come. It can remind us of where we fit on the time line of human achievement, an ultimate value of art.

Wynton Marsalis

The United States is a giant island of freedom, achievement, wealth and prosperity in a world hostile to our values.

Phyllis Schlafly

That's what makes the Ryder Cup in golf so much better than the Masters or the U.S. Open. To be a part of something that is not about personal achievement, but about representing everyone and sharing it with the whole country, it's wonderful.

Scott Hamilton

I got my first lifetime achievement award years ago, and I was very excited, but then I got a sense of: Well, can one get a second lifetime award?

Michael Palin

Don't confuse honours with achievement.

Zadie Smith

It seemed romantic but also tragic - people would be winning but then lose it all, or crash but fight on, break bones but get back on their bikes and try to finish. Just getting to the end was seen as an achievement in itself.

David Millar

An egalitarian educational system is necessarily opposed to meritocracy and reward for achievement. It is inevitably opposed to procedures that might reveal differing levels of achievement.

Robert Bork

Fact is, awards shows were never really about recognizing achievement. They were a publicity ploy cooked up in the late 1920s by MGM topper Louie Mayer and his newly formed Academy of Motion Picture Arts and Sciences which was itself, back in the day, nothing but a front organization to discourage unionizing.

John Ridley

The fact that monasticism preceded the identification of greed as a primal sin is an important reminder that our very ability to name sin is a theological achievement.

Stanley Hauerwas

I don't get recognised that much yet in London, but when I do I get a real sense of achievement.

Idris Elba

Simply racing a Formula 1 car is an achievement.

Sebastian Vettel

Art is a critical component in a well-rounded education. Art is the level playing field - no matter how rich or poor, tall or short, pretty or ugly to the bone, if you can draw, you can find personal fulfillment and build self-confidence. Art is the highest achievement of mankind.

Lynda Resnick

I love the song 'Into the Night.' It's Roy Orbison meets David Lynch meets Iggy Pop on amphetamines. It has a punk edge that is not HIM, per se. It is super melodic and super '60s, and that is very new to me and it is a sense of achievement to me.

Ville Valo

It is time to celebrate the New Black Americans - those who have sealed the Deal, who aren't beholden to liberal indulgence any more than they are to the disdain of the hard Right. It is time to praise blacks who are merely undeniable in their individuality and exemplary in their levels of achievement.

John Ridley

My concentration was really on getting to university and becoming a doctor. My parents let me know that school marks were important. Achievement was something which came by hard work.

Roger Bannister

I think protecting your family and giving to them is so important. It's the most important achievement.

Natalia Vodianova

In Japan, mothers insist on achievement and accomplishment as a sign of love and respect. Thus to fail places children in a highly shamed situation.

Michael Lewis

I don't know what makes someone hip. The goal is artist achievement and the best work we can do with no limitation.

Rick Rubin

The most important thing to strive for in life is some kind of personal and professional achievement. Not as a man or a woman, but as a person.

Candace Bushnell

Celebrate your child's achievement, then rotate it when the next mini-masterpiece comes along. Then chuck the old picture. Don't worry that you're throwing away a memory. Your children will remember your praise more than they will remember the picture with macaroni and glitter glued on it.

Niecy Nash

Something happens when you become an elder rock & roller and you're still functioning. People start to give you awards and recognize achievements. It's the life achievement period of your career.

Geddy Lee

Workaholics typically have a lot of achievement with very little appreciation of what they have, whether it's cars or friendships or otherwise. That is a shallow victory. Then you have people with a lot of appreciation and no achievement, which is fine, but it doesn't create a lot of good in the world.

Timothy Ferriss

It seems like every year Hollywood makes an attempt to retell the Manson story, and I just couldn't be less interested in it. It's not really our crowning achievement as a civilisation. I'm not saying it shouldn't be done, but it just bores me.

John Hawkes

Freedom is an internal achievement rather than an external adjustment.

Powell Clayton

Chess is a sport. The main object in the game of chess remains the achievement of victory.

Max Euwe

We have a chance to wind down and expedite the removal of 96 percent of the world's nuclear weapons. What an achievement it would be, if at the end of the next administration, we could say that the nuclear arsenals of both Russia and the United States had been reduced to the barest minimums.

Dianne Feinstein

I played college soccer before I was hurt, and just to be able to jump back into something that you could be so competitive at or you can achieve, to get to the Paralympics, that's the first really big achievement that you can have. It's the second biggest sporting event in the world. To be a part of it and to get a medal for that, it's unreal.

Mark Zupan

www.ingramcontent.com/pod-product-compliance
Lightning Source LLC
Chambersburg PA
CBHW071239280526
45787CB00002B/995